The Collaborative CODER

Building Software in Distributed Remote Teams

Amarachukwu Nwandu

Globally Available

Published in Nigeria, 2020
Emphaloz Publishing House

A catalogue record for this book is available at the National Library of Nigeria

Table Of Contents

Preface

In an era where borders are digital and offices are optional, the way we build software has evolved beyond imagination. The traditional model of developers huddled in the same room, sketching ideas on whiteboards, has given way to a dynamic, global ecosystem of remote collaboration. From solo freelancers in coffee shops to tightly coordinated teams spread across continents; the modern coder is no longer confined by geography but empowered by it.

Foreword

The world of software development has always been driven by change: new languages, new frameworks, and new challenges. But perhaps the most transformative shift in recent years hasn't been technological; it's been cultural. The rise of distributed, remote teams has fundamentally altered how we write code, solve problems, and bring ideas to life. I've had the privilege of working with remote teams across time zones and cultures, and I've seen firsthand how collaboration, when done right, becomes a powerful force. But I've also witnessed the friction, miscommunications, workflow mismatches, and the loneliness that can come from working apart. This book, The Collaborative Coder, is a timely and necessary guide to navigating those very realities.

Introduction

The software industry has undergone a fundamental transformation, one that has untethered it from the confines of physical office spaces and traditional nine-to-five routines. What began as a temporary adjustment during global disruption has since become a defining feature of modern software development. Developers from different countries, continents, and time zones work together to build, ship, and maintain products without ever meeting in person. Remote work is no longer a backup plan; it is now an operational norm adopted by startups, tech behemoths, and open-source communities alike.

However, working remotely in the software industry is far more complex than simply opening a laptop from the comfort of your own home. It necessitates a thorough rethinking of how we communicate, share knowledge, manage codebases, and promote alignment across distributed teams. Collaboration in this new environment must be deliberate, not accidental. Culture must be intentionally fostered, rather than left to casual hallway conversations. Trust must be built through clarity, consistency, and empathy, not proximity or supervision. Even the metrics we use to define productivity and success have evolved, with an emphasis on output, team synergy, and autonomy rather than visibility and presence.

The Collaborative Coder is a response to this global shift and an investigation into how remote software teams can thrive in an environment where face-to-face interaction is uncommon but the need for connection, culture, and creativity persists. This book explores the practical and human challenges of working in remote-first environments. It provides strategies for creating strong workflows, establishing clear communication norms, and maintaining high-performance team dynamics while preserving empathy, innovation, and a sense of belonging.

Whether you're a developer navigating asynchronous workflows, a team leader attempting to foster cohesion across time zones, a manager rethinking how to measure and mentor from afar, or a startup founder building a company without borders, The Collaborative Coder speaks directly to your experience. It's not enough to simply survive the era of distributed work; you must also master it and turn remote collaboration into a competitive advantage.

Chapter One

Rethinking Collaboration in a Remote World

The story of modern software development is, in many ways, the story of unlearning old assumptions. For decades, productivity in tech was equated with physical presence. The measure of a committed engineer was someone visible at their desk, attending meetings in person, and available for spontaneous collaboration at any moment. Offices became cultural hubs places where productivity, camaraderie, and creativity were expected to intersect naturally. But today, this model is being fundamentally redefined. The rise of the remote developer is not a trend it is a transformation. It's not merely a change in location, but a rethinking of what makes great software teams succeed. This shift challenges the ingrained belief that proximity breeds productivity and replaces it with a more nuanced philosophy: results over rituals, clarity over constant contact, and communication over control.

Although the shift to remote work may seem sudden to some, especially in the wake of the global pandemic, its roots stretch back decades. Tools like Git made distribution control not just possible but reliable. Cloud infrastructure allowed applications to be deployed and managed from anywhere. Messaging and documentation tools began replacing office whiteboards and sticky notes with real-time updates and searchable archives. Slowly but steadily, the groundwork was being laid. Then came the global disruption of COVID-19, a crisis that forced organizations to reimagine work overnight. What began as an emergency measure to protect public health evolved into a large-scale realization: many software teams not only *could* work remotely but also thrive remotely. Since then, we've seen a new era emerge, where remote work is no longer the exception or a perk for selecting employees but a strategic choice that defines how entire companies operate.

The early image of successful teams sitting shoulder-to-shoulder in high-energy office environments has given way to a more fluid, global reality. Teams now span time zones and continents. Success is no longer defined by hours spent in a meeting room but by the clarity of written communication, the efficiency of asynchronous workflows, and the ability of individuals to take ownership of outcomes. A high-performing team today is not one that shares a floor plan but one that shares a vision, a rhythm, and a sense of mutual respect. The remote developer represents more than just someone working from home. They are a part of a global movement that values autonomy, purpose, and impact over visibility. They contribute to systems where knowledge is open, communication is intentional, and flexibility is not a trade-off for productivity but a catalyst for it. This shift is not simply a matter of convenience or cost it's a new operating model for building great software in a globally connected world.

Tools as Infrastructure: The Technological Backbone of Distributed Collaboration

The success of remote development is not just the result of changing attitudes; it's the product of evolving infrastructure. In the office era, physical proximity served as the invisible glue holding teams together. Without realizing it, developers relied on shared screens, overheard conversations, and impromptu discussions to stay aligned. In a remote environment, that invisible glue must be replaced with something more intentional, scalable, and resilient: a robust stack of digital tools and integrated systems.

At the center of this new infrastructure are collaboration platforms designed to replicate and, in many cases, improve the coordination previously achieved in person. Tools like GitHub enable developers to collaborate on the same codebase regardless of where they are in the world. Pull requests allow for thoughtful, asynchronous code reviews. Branching strategies make parallel development not only possible but practical. Issues and discussions document decision-making, giving everyone a historical context that outlives transient conversations.

Slack, Microsoft Teams, and similar platforms offer real-time communication channels tailored to the dynamic needs of development teams. But their effectiveness lies not just in speed; it's in how teams use them. A message in Slack can be more thoughtful and inclusive than a hasty in-person conversation. Channels can be created for different topics, departments, or initiatives, reducing noise and improving focus. Paired with integrations from CI/CD tools, deployment systems, and error trackers, these platforms become the real-time control room of a modern development workflow.

Meanwhile, Notion, Confluence, and Coda have redefined documentation. Where once documentation was an afterthought, a stale Word doc buried in a network drive, it is now a living resource. These tools allow teams to create wikis, share updates, track roadmaps, and onboard new team members with clarity and structure. Remote-first organizations treat documentation as part of the product itself, ensuring decisions are visible, onboarding is repeatable, and processes are not siloed within individual minds.

Video conferencing tools like Zoom, Google Meet, and Whereby replace the need for physical meeting rooms but with greater flexibility. Remote stand-ups, sprint planning sessions, and retrospectives can still occur, just more focused and deliberate. Screen-sharing, session recording, and shared whiteboarding tools add even more richness than what's available in traditional settings.

When all of these tools are connected through automation and cleaning processes, the result is an ecosystem where distributed development is not only viable it's optimized. Notifications flow automatically. Code is deployed with confidence. Work is tracked transparently. Teams know who's doing what, when, and why not because they overheard it, but because it's been designed into the system.

The most successful remote teams don't just adopt these tools; they orchestrate them. They think of tools as extensions of their culture. They design workflows that minimize friction and maximize clarity. In doing so, they create an environment that is not only productive but also resilient, even when people are scattered across the globe.

Culture Without Walls: The Human Blueprint for Distributed Success

Beyond tools and processes lies something even more essential: culture. For any software team, culture is an invisible operating system. It governs how people treat each other, how they resolve conflict, how they celebrate wins, and how they show up when things get hard. In remote teams, culture doesn't disappear, but it must be cultivated more intentionally. In co-located teams, culture often forms organically. Shared lunches, casual Friday drinks, and overheard conversations all of these informal interactions contribute to a sense of belonging. But in remote teams, there are no watercoolers. There are no visual cues to tell when someone is struggling. That absence of physical presence means that what used to happen casually now has to happen *deliberately*.

Communication in remote teams isn't spontaneous; it's designed. Trust isn't based on visibility; it's based on follow-through. Feedback isn't whispered in a hallway; it's written down with care. In a distributed environment, culture is built through rituals, not routines. It's embedded in how teams write documentation, how leaders respond to mistakes, and how everyone treats asynchronous communication as an equal citizen to live meetings. Strong remote cultures don't happen by accident; they are architected. Teams that thrive remotely develop shared agreements around communication, time zone expectations, meeting frequency, and even response times. They define what success looks like and how it's celebrated. They invest in psychological safety by encouraging open questions, normalizing vulnerability, and making space for personal connection. This doesn't mean trying to replicate every in-office ritual online. Remote culture is not about creating virtual happy hours just to simulate "togetherness." It's about building new forms of connection that respect people's space, time, and individuality. It's about making sure every voice is heard, especially when it's easy to disappear behind a muted mic or delayed reply. And it's about valuing what each person brings to the team, not based on how loud or visible they are, but on how meaningfully they contribute.

Of course, remote work introduces real challenges. Time zone mismatches can stretch communication. Onboarding can feel impersonal. Isolation can lead to burnout if not addressed proactively. These are not trivial problems, but they are solvable. And when solved well, they often lead to better outcomes than the traditional model. Clearer documentation. Stronger onboarding systems. More thoughtful communication. Deeper empathy. In the end, the goal is not to mimic the in-office experience but to surpass it. To create teams that are more inclusive, more sustainable, and more adaptable. Teams where the culture isn't confined to a building but lives in the shared behaviors, values, and commitments of the people who build software together from anywhere in the world.

Chapter Two

Foundations of Trust and Communication

In remote software teams, trust is not a luxury; it's a necessity. It's the invisible architecture holding everything else in place. Without shared spaces or daily face-to-face interaction, teams cannot rely on casual conversations, body language, or the energy of co-location to form bonds. In this distributed environment, trust must be visible, intentional, and actively sustained. In co-located teams, trust tends to grow organically. You learn someone's habits by observing them daily. You share jokes in the break room, troubleshoot bugs together on a whiteboard, or catch someone's mood just by watching their expressions in a meeting. Remote teams don't have those cues. They work behind screens, often in different time zones, with cultural and linguistic nuances that shape their interactions. That's why, in remote teams, trust is built through behavior, not proximity. Reliability becomes one of the most crucial indicators of trust. When someone says they'll complete a task by Friday and follows through, they're sending a clear message: You can count on me. When delays happen (as they inevitably do) and they're communicated early with context, that transparency fosters even deeper confidence. These consistent behaviors create a culture where people feel seen, respected, and interdependent even when they've never met in person.

But trust doesn't exist in a vacuum. It thrives best in environments where empathy is present. Working remotely means that teammates may have different home environments, cultural holidays, caregiving responsibilities, or time zone constraints. Understanding that someone might not be online when you are or that they prefer asynchronous feedback requires emotional maturity. It requires grace. Without empathy, assumptions take root: that someone is disengaged because they respond slowly or unskilled because they're quiet. Remote teams that understand and respect personal contexts develop more inclusive and durable relationships.

The most successful remote teams practice psychological safety, which allows people to speak up, ask questions, and admit gaps in knowledge without fear of embarrassment or backlash. Trust, once established in this way, becomes a powerful engine. It speeds up decision-making, reduces micromanagement, and enables more autonomous workflows. Trust is not just about being nice; it directly impacts how effectively software gets built.

Intentional Communication: The Lifeline of Distributed Work

In remote development, communication is more than a tool; it's the lifeline of every decision, task, and collaboration. When developers, product managers, and designers are scattered across the globe, the ability to express thoughts clearly and interpret others accurately becomes essential. Unlike in-person settings, where tone, facial expressions, and body language support communication, remote teams rely almost entirely on written and verbal clarity. This makes communication not just important but mission critical. Clarity is the most valuable currency in distributed teams. Vague messages create confusion. Long, meandering explanations waste time. Overly terse replies can be misinterpreted as rude or dismissive. That's why remote professionals must cultivate the skill of writing with precision and purpose. A well-written Slack message or pull request review can do more to advance a project than a one-hour meeting. Clarity doesn't mean dumbing things down; it means making your ideas easier for others to engage in.

Writing, in remote settings, becomes your voice. It's how you represent your thoughts, track decisions, explain your code, or deliver feedback. Good writing improves velocity, transparency, and shared understanding. Poor writing leads to misunderstandings, rework, and unnecessary meetings. Remote developers should treat writing like any other professional skill: practice it, edit it, and approach it with care. Break down complex thoughts into manageable parts. Lead with what's important. Always read your message from the perspective of someone who might be tired, distracted, or in another country. Equally important is understanding when to use asynchronous vs. synchronous communication. Asynchronous tools such as Notion, GitHub, Loom, or Slack threads allow people to work on their own schedules. This is especially vital when your team spans multiple time zones. Async communication promotes deep work, reduces the pressure of instant replies, and creates a written trail of decisions and discussions. But it's not a silver bullet.

Some conversations require real-time interaction, especially those involving brainstorming, urgent problem-solving, or sensitive emotional nuance. Synchronous tools like Zoom, Google Meet, or live Slack huddles create immediacy, intimacy, and alignment. The most effective teams don't rigidly choose one style over the other. Instead, they learn to calibrate their communication tools to the task at hand, balancing async efficiency with sync empathy. Tone also matters, especially in writing. Without vocal tone or facial cues, it's easy for feedback to feel harsh or dismissive. That's why it's essential to write with warmth and clarity, particularly when offering constructive feedback. Be specific. Be respectful. Focus on the work, not the person. Equally important is recognizing good work out loud. Remote teams that regularly praise effort and progress create a stronger sense of motivation and belonging.

Designing Communication Culture: Systems That Empower, Not Overwhelm

A remote team's communication culture doesn't build itself. It must be designed with the same intention as any product or system. Great communication is not just about choosing the right words; it's about choosing the right tools, routines, norms, and expectations that help people stay connected and aligned without feeling overwhelmed.

First, remote teams must establish clear protocols. What tools are used for what purpose? Where does documentation live? How are updates shared? What's the expected response time for async communication? Without clear agreements, people default to their own habits, which leads to misalignment and frustration. For example, using Slack for urgent issues, Notion for documentation, and GitHub for code discussions ensures that each channel serves its purpose and reduces noise. But good communication also means creating space for connection. Remote teams can feel transactional if every interaction is work focused. Building camaraderie requires opportunities for social interaction. Casual Slack channels, virtual coffee chats, team games, and even asynchronous icebreakers can create moments of joy and bonding. These aren't distractions; they're investments in team resilience. One common misconception is that remote teams must "overcommunicate." While transparency is critical, overcommunication doesn't mean spamming every channel with every thought. Instead, it means being proactive when context shifts. If a deadline is moving, if a dependency changes, or if feedback is needed, communicate early and clearly. Conversely, be mindful of creating digital clutter. Ask yourself: Does this message help someone do their job better or feel more connected? If not, maybe it doesn't need to be sent.

Feedback is another pillar of a healthy communication culture. Without the nuance of facial expressions and voice inflections, feedback must be crafted with even greater intentionality. Focus on impact, not character. Suggest alternatives, not just critique. And just as importantly, celebrate wins, no matter how small. A quick thank-you or shout-out can transform morale in a way that data dashboards or burndown charts never will. Ultimately, a healthy remote communication culture is purpose-driven, human-centered, and flexible. It aligns everyone toward common goals while respecting individual work styles and life rhythms. When remote teams get communication right, they don't just eliminate the pain points of distance; they unlock new possibilities for collaboration, innovation, and belonging.

Chapter Three

Tools That Enable, Habits That Sustain

Given how digital the world is becoming, it's simple to assume that effective remote development teams rely heavily on their technology stack. Any team can work efficiently from any location if they have the proper code sharing, video conferencing, project tracking, and messaging tools. After all, developers can write, test, deploy, and collaborate on software from anywhere in the world thanks to these tools. However, while tools are undoubtedly useful, they are not the heart of a successful remote team. Tools enable collaboration, but it is the habits of those who use them that make it productive and sustainable. The difference between a struggling remote team and a thriving one is often determined by how they use the tools. Technology has the potential to bring people together, but without discipline, structure, and shared practices, it can also lead to chaos. Communication becomes fragmented. Tasks got untracked. Important information gets buried. Meetings multiply without producing clarity. In short, progress slows, accountability weakens, and morale drops. To truly thrive as a collaborative remote developer, it is not enough to simply adopt the right tools. What matters more is developing the right habits in how those tools are used consistently, respectfully, and purposefully.

Thoughtful Tool Selection Is the Foundation, Not the Goal

The number of digital tools available to remote development teams today is overwhelming. There are dozens of apps available to help a distributed team with version control, task management, communication, time tracking, and documentation. The sheer number of options can lead one to believe that using more tools is the only solution. However, the most effective teams do not rely on a constantly expanding toolkit. They make careful, deliberate decisions based on their workflow, team size, and primary goals.

Great teams choose a focused, intentional set of tools that support the way they work, rather than forcing them to adapt to a tool's limitations or quirks. The most important quality in a toolset isn't popularity or feature count, but how well the tools integrate and create a coherent, navigable system. Tools should reduce complexity, not add to it. Communication platforms should connect smoothly with task trackers and code repositories. Documentation systems should be easy to update and even easier to search. When a developer wants to know the status of a task, where to find a feature spec, or how to deploy a service, they shouldn't have to ask around or dig through email threads; they should know exactly where to look.

Clarity is everything in a remote setting. With everyone working asynchronously and often across time zones, there's no room for ambiguity about where information lives or how work gets tracked. This is why integration matters more than feature count. A project management tool that seamlessly links to code branches, commit messages, and pull requests will do more for productivity than any number of standalone dashboards. And more importantly, once a tool is chosen, it must be used consistently. Even the most powerful platform is useless if some people use it one way, others use it differently, and many don't use it at all. A tool becomes valuable only when its use is predictable.

It is not enough to simply have a shared project board. The board must be kept up to date. Tasks must be clearly named, categorized, and moved through a meaningful workflow. Similarly, version control systems do not automatically foster collaboration; they do so only when developers adhere to agreed-upon conventions for branch naming, commit message writing, and pull request management. Communication tools do not automatically create transparency; how people use channels, threads, and status updates determines their effectiveness. A remote team that agrees on how to use each tool can operate efficiently and clearly. A team that lacks this agreement risks drowning in digital noise.

Habits That Foster a High-Trust Remote Culture

Remote collaboration is sustained by habit. Behind every successful team is a set of daily, weekly, and project-based behaviors that keep everyone aligned, informed, and moving forward. These behaviors are often invisible to the outside world, but they serve as the foundation for all visible output. And, while tools may facilitate these behaviors, they cannot create them. For example, a culture of writing detailed commit messages demonstrates a team's dedication to maintainability and accountability. It demonstrates that developers aren't just working for the present; they're thinking about the future, about the next person who needs to read or revise their code. Similarly, when developers open pull requests with thoughtful descriptions, clear tests instructions, and tagged reviewers, they respect the time and attention of their teammates. They're not just checking a box; they're enabling smooth, respectful collaboration. These are habits, not features.

Good habits also extend to task management. Updating task status regularly, clarifying scope, estimating effort, and closing completed items may sound simple, but doing these things consistently can transform the way a team functions. It ensures that everyone has a shared understanding of progress, workload, and blockers. It removes the need for micromanagement and constant follow-ups. It creates visibility across the team, regardless of where people are located. Communication habits are equally critical. In a co-located team, casual check-ins and informal knowledge sharing happen naturally. In a remote team, they must be recreated intentionally. This means having structured communication practices such as daily check-ins, clear ownership of decisions, and a default to documenting discussions. It means recognizing when to use asynchronous messages versus real-time meetings and always capturing key decisions in writing. Documentation, in particular, becomes the remote team's lifeline. It replaces the in-person explanations, the whiteboard sessions, and the side-of-desk coaching that often happens in physical offices. But documentation is only useful if it is treated as a living part of the workflow, not a static archive. High-functioning remote teams write guides as they work, update documents when processes change, and structure their documentation so that it is easy to read, search, and update.

Good documentation habits have cascading benefits. They reduce repeated questions, speed up onboarding, and help preserve institutional knowledge. They also foster a culture of transparency. When a team takes the time to explain how something works or why a decision was made, they create trust. When changes are documented and shared openly, it signals respect for others' time and curiosity. These small acts build a collaborative spirit over time. Remote work also demands habits that support well-being, not just productivity. Respecting working hours, limiting meeting length, reviewing code promptly, and acknowledging contributions are not just good practices; they are expressions of care. They show that people are seen, heard, and valued. And they help reduce the emotional fatigue that can accumulate when working in isolation. These habits might seem subtle, but they're what turn a collection of individuals into a cohesive team.

Avoiding Tool Overload and Keeping Collaboration Simple

One of the most common mistakes remote teams make is falling into the trap of tool overload. When a problem emerges, delays in communication, missing tasks, unclear ownership are tempting to assume that the right app will fix it. Add a new tracker. Install another integration. Subscribe to a new notification system. But this mindset often leads to diminishing returns. Instead of solving the problem, more tools often create new ones.

Every tool adds complexity. It must be learned, configured, maintained, and woven into existing workflows. It generates notifications, stores information, and requires attention. The more tools a team uses, the more fragmented its knowledge becomes. Conversations happen across multiple platforms. Files get stored in multiple locations. Tasks are duplicated or lost. Onboarding new team members becomes a scavenger hunt. And before long, the team spends more time managing its tools than doing actual work. The most effective remote teams are not the ones using the most tools; they're the ones using the fewest tools *well*. They focus on clarity, not coverage. They value consistency over novelty. And when a new tool is introduced, they do so intentionally, with a clear plan for adoption, training, and ongoing use.

Simplifying the tool stack has powerful benefits. It reduces context switching. It sharpens focus. It ensures that everyone knows where to go, what to do, and how to contribute. It fosters a sense of stability and predictability, essential qualities in a distributed team. And it creates space for the team to focus on habits, relationships, and results, rather than chasing every new productivity trend. When a remote team avoids tool overload, aligns on how tools are used, and reinforces good habits through every interaction, they create something rare: a calm, clear, and collaborative environment where people can do their best work together, even from afar. In the end, remote collaboration is not just a technical system; it's a human one. The tools are important. But the habits are everything.

Chapter Four

Managing Time Zones and Work Rhythms

When you enter the world of remote software development, one of the first and most fundamental shifts you'll notice is the way time works. In a traditional co-located office environment, time is measured by the familiar rhythms of a shared space: the morning buzz of coffee-fueled standups, spontaneous hallway discussions, late-afternoon check-ins, and the sense that everyone is operating under a similar schedule. But in a distributed team, those rhythms disappear. Time no longer runs on a single clock. It fragments. Developers stretch across continents. One team member starts their day in Melbourne just as another in Vancouver is heading to bed. Morning updates for one person arrive hours after someone else has already logged off. At first glance, this asynchronous reality might feel like an obstacle, an ever-present logistical puzzle that delays decision-making and slows down progress. But in truth, when approached with intention, empathy, and strategy, this time zone diversity becomes one of the most powerful features of remote work.

Global teams have the potential to operate continuously, handing off work in an elegant chain that resembles a relay race more than a traditional workday. While one engineer wraps up a new feature in Lagos, another in New York wakes up to review the pull request, and a third in Tokyo can handle testing and deployment. This model, often referred to as "follow-the-sun" development, offers near-constant momentum. But it doesn't happen by accident. It requires a fundamental redesign of how teams communicate, plan, and collaborate.

Navigating Time Zones with Intention and Empathy

The true challenge of working across time zones isn't merely about clock differences; it's about aligning workflows, expectations, and team culture around those differences. When remote teams ignore time zone disparities and try to operate as if everyone is still in the same office, frustration quickly sets in. Conversations get delayed, decisions stagnate, and people begin to feel excluded or left behind. Developers end up waiting hours or even days for answers to simple questions, only to find that progress has stalled during the gap.

Time zones directly impact everything from feedback loops to inclusion in decision-making. They shape not only how work gets done but also how connected people feel to the team. Let's consider two fictional developers: Priya in Mumbai and Marco in São Paulo. Their workdays only overlap for about one hour. Without intentional structure, they might struggle to stay aligned. One pushes code and waits for a review. The other misses the update and begins working on something else. The cycle of waiting and missing continues, leading to wasted effort and mutual frustration. But if the team prioritizes asynchronous collaboration, this limited overlap becomes less of a barrier and more of a rhythm. When Priya finishes her work for the day, she writes a clear update, documents her reasoning, and hands it off through the team's shared tools. Marco begins his day with all the context he needs to review, contribute, or move things forward. The baton gets passed cleanly not through rushed meetings, but through deliberate communication and well-established practices. This approach demands a new mindset. Teams that succeed in navigating time zones treat them not as roadblocks but as parameters in a system they can design around. They plan their workflows so that progress isn't dependent on real-time interaction. They document decisions as they're made, communicate proactively, and schedule meetings sparingly only when truly necessary and when overlapping availability allows.

Designing for time zone equity also means resisting the urge to center one region as the "default." It's common, especially in North American or European-based companies, to anchor meeting schedules around one primary time zone, forcing colleagues elsewhere to adapt repeatedly. Over time, this creates resentment and fatigue. Instead, inclusive teams rotate meeting times, ensure key discussions are documented, and make asynchronous input just as valid as live participation. This intentionality extends beyond meetings. Deadlines, too, should reflect time zone awareness. A Friday 5 p.m. deadline in London might fall in the middle of the night for a team member in Seoul. Teams that build with empathy consider local holidays, weekends, and working hours before locking in deliverables. Time differences are not just logistical; they are deeply human. Respecting them is not a courtesy. It is a requirement for fairness and functionality in distributed collaboration.

Asynchronous Communication: The Cornerstone of Global Collaboration

The most powerful tool a distributed team can adopt isn't a piece of software; it's a philosophy: defaulting to asynchronous communication. In this mode of working, updates, questions, decisions, and reviews don't rely on people being online at the same moment. Instead, information is clearly written, structured, and shared so others can respond in their own time, without delay or confusion. Asynchronous workflows demand clarity. When teams embrace this model, they become better at writing. Tasks are written with full context and clear expectations. Project updates are thorough, not vague. Comments on pull requests explain not just what changed but why it changed. The entire team benefits because knowledge becomes durable. It's not locked in a chat thread or a meeting that someone missed, it's available, searchable, and referenceable.

Take code reviews as an example. In a co-located team, it might be common to hop into a conference room or screen-share to walk someone through a new feature. But in a distributed team, reviews happen via comments and commits. The developer leaving feedback might be nine hours ahead of the person who wrote the code. This separation isn't a disadvantage; it's an opportunity. It gives both people time to think deeply, leave precise notes, and avoid rushed decisions. The result is often better quality, not just better flexibility. Sprint planning also benefits from asynchronous preparation. Rather than dragging everyone into a call that fits poorly into half the team's calendars, product managers and engineers can review tasks, weigh priorities, and propose ideas in shared documents or planning boards before the actual meeting. When the team does meet ideally during overlapping hours, the discussion can be shorter, more focused, and grounded in pre-read material.

Documentation becomes central to all of this. For asynchronous work to thrive, documentation must be seen not as a byproduct of "real" work but as an integral part of it. Whether it's onboarding guides, architectural diagrams, or decision logs, good documentation helps people onboard faster, avoid redundant questions, and stay aligned even when they're continents apart. It also reinforces a culture of transparency where knowledge is shared, not hoarded, and contributions are visible, not hidden behind timezone walls. The move toward asynchronous work also creates healthier, more inclusive team dynamics. It shifts the emphasis from who can respond the fastest to who can contribute the most thoughtfully. It respects introverts, deep thinkers, and people with caregiving responsibilities or unconventional schedules. It helps everyone do their best work not just the most visible work.

Supporting Human Rhythms in a Nonlinear Workday

Time zones, at their core, are not just about time; they are about energy. Every individual has their own biological rhythm. Some team members hit a peak in productivity early in the morning. Others are night owls who write their best code after dark. Distributed work gives people the ability to match their work hours to their personal energy cycles, but only if the team culture allows it. This freedom requires trust. It requires moving away from the outdated mindset that equates productivity with visibility. Just because you can't see someone online at 10 a.m. doesn't mean they're not working hard, it may just mean their peak focus time is elsewhere. High-performing remote teams evaluate outcomes, not online presence. They trust people to manage their time in a way that's effective for both them and the team.

Some teams implement "core hours," a designated period where all team members are expected to be available for real-time collaboration. These hours are chosen based on the maximum possible overlap between time zones. Outside of that window, individuals are free to structure their day according to their needs. This hybrid model provides both flexibility and predictability.

But even core hours must be approached thoughtfully. If they disproportionately burden team members in certain locations, forcing someone to join daily meetings at 10 p.m., they're not really fair. The best teams share the load. They rotate meeting times, provide recordings with notes, and empower team members to contribute asynchronously when live attendance isn't feasible. Equally important is guarding against the "always-on" culture that remote work can accidentally foster. In global teams where messages arrive around the clock, there's often an implicit pressure to respond immediately, even outside of working hours. This blurs the line between personal and professional time, leading to fatigue and eventual burnout.

To counter this, teams must explicitly set norms that protect boundaries. Status indicators should reflect true availability. Scheduled send features should be encouraged, allowing people to write updates when it's convenient for them, without pinging others during off-hours. Most importantly, teams must communicate that delayed responses are not only acceptable they are expected.

Tagging someone in a message doesn't mean "drop everything." It simply means "this needs your input when you're back." When this expectation is reinforced through leadership behavior, documentation, and everyday practice, it creates a healthier, more humane culture. One where people feel empowered to rest, recharge, and return with fresh focus. When teams operate this way by respecting rhythms, designing with empathy, and using asynchronous tools well, they transform time zones from a logistical constraint into a strategic asset. They don't fight time; they coordinate with it. They don't chase productivity; they pass it forward, day by day, hand by hand. The most resilient remote development teams aren't trying to replicate the office. They are redesigning collaboration for a world without walls or clocks.

They understand that time, when approached with empathy and structure, becomes a powerful tool for innovation. They prioritize written clarity over spoken urgency. They respect energy as much as availability. And they build cultures where work doesn't depend on being present but on being purposeful.

In these teams, productivity isn't interrupted by distance. It flows. Like a well-practiced relay, one team member finishes a sprint and hands off the baton to the next. Each knows their role. Each trusts the other. The race isn't against time; it's with it.

Chapter Five

Effective Remote Leadership

Leadership in remote teams is fundamentally different from traditional, in-person management. It demands a shift in mindset, where the focus moves away from authority and control and toward influence, clarity, trust, and emotional presence. In a distributed environment, you can't lead by proximity or presence alone. Your leadership must be felt through the systems you build, the tone you set, and the culture you create. Physical presence is replaced by intentional communication. Daily visibility is replaced by reliable, predictable support. And micromanagement gives way to empowerment, structure, and trust. In remote teams, what defines a great leader is not their ability to monitor work in real time, but their ability to design a framework where people can do their best work independently and know they are supported while doing it. The most effective remote leaders cultivate clarity, foster autonomy, and remain deeply human, showing up not just with strategy but with empathy.

This kind of leadership isn't accidental. It requires deliberate effort, consistent habits, and emotional intelligence. It's about being accessible without being overbearing, communicative without being performative, and emotionally present without micromanaging. Let's explore the three pillars of exceptional remote leadership: communication and clarity, trust and visibility, and emotional presence.

Communication and Clarity: The Engine of Remote Leadership

In a traditional office setting, a lot of communication happens informally. A manager might stop by a desk to clarify an objective, or a team member might overhear a conversation that provides useful context. Remote work erases these opportunities for ambient awareness. In their absence, leaders must become intentional architects of clarity. This starts with how goals, expectations, and progress are communicated. Clear direction is no longer optional, it is foundational. A remote leader must articulate not just what needs to be done, but why it matters, how success will be measured, and what timeline is expected. This level of clarity doesn't stifle creativity, it enables it. When expectations are well-defined, people are free to take initiative without fear of misalignment.

Leaders also need to ensure that communication flows in both directions. It's not enough to broadcast instructions and updates. A strong remote leader creates mechanisms for feedback, questions, and open discussion. That means holding regular one-on-ones, hosting weekly team updates, and ensuring there are written records of decisions, timelines, and goals. Documentation is a powerful ally in remote environments. It gives the team a shared source of truth that reduces confusion, accelerates onboarding, and ensures that no one is left guessing. Moreover, remote leaders must learn to communicate asynchronously and with care. They recognize that not all team members will be online at the same time, so they provide thoughtful updates, leave detailed comments, and prepare materials in advance of meetings. They avoid last-minute surprises and give people the time and context they need to contribute effectively. This includes being explicit about priorities, outlining deliverables in written form, and encouraging the team to document key work decisions. One hallmark of great remote leadership is the ability to create systems that reduce the need for constant supervision. When a team has access to a well-structured roadmap, a clear set of responsibilities, and defined channels for updates and feedback, they don't need to rely on spontaneous check-ins. This reduces decision fatigue and makes the team more resilient. Everyone knows what's expected of them, and they know how to ask for support when needed.

In remote settings, communication is also how leadership presence is maintained. Leaders are not visible by sitting at the head of the table they are visible by consistently showing up in meaningful ways: responding to updates, asking thoughtful questions, reinforcing values, and celebrating progress. In a virtual workspace, silence from leadership can easily be interpreted as disinterest. That's why remote leaders must err on the side of presence, especially when it comes to positive reinforcement. Regular praise, gratitude, and acknowledgment go a long way in building morale and momentum when your team is separated by distance.

Clarity, in the end, is not about overexplaining; it's about creating the conditions where everyone knows what matters, why it matters, and how they can contribute meaningfully. That is the true foundation of leadership in a distributed world.

Trust and Visibility Leading Without Micromanagement

One of the most defining challenges of remote leadership is learning to lead without control. In the absence of physical visibility, some leaders fall into the trap of surveillance, trying to measure productivity by activity logs, message counts, or online status. But this approach is not only unsustainable, it's counterproductive. It undermines trust, stifles initiative, and fosters a culture of fear. Remote teams thrive when trust is the default, not something that must be earned with constant proof. Great leaders understand that they cannot and should not try to monitor every detail. Instead, they create systems that provide visibility without intrusion. Progress is made transparent through structured check-ins, project updates, dashboards, and shared planning tools. This kind of visibility isn't about control; it's about shared accountability.

When a team knows what others are working on, where blockers exist, and how decisions are being made, they feel more connected and aligned. They don't need to be told what to do; they see where things are going and where they fit into the broader picture. This autonomy builds both confidence and efficiency. Trust in remote teams also manifests in how leaders treat time. Rather than equating productivity with hours spent online, great leaders focus on outcomes. They trust that their team members will structure their days in ways that optimize focus and performance even if that means working non-traditional hours or stepping away during the day to recharge. This flexibility is not a risk to be managed; it's a benefit to be embraced. It gives people the freedom to work in alignment with their own rhythms, which often leads to better creativity and sustained motivation. However, trust does not mean total detachment. Great leaders remain engaged and available. They check in without hovering, offer support without imposing, and stay connected to both the work and the people behind it. They ask thoughtful questions, review progress regularly, and coach their team members toward growth. The difference is that they do it from a place of partnership, not control.

Another key part of building trust is consistency. In remote settings, inconsistency is amplified. If a leader responds to some people and ignores others, it's noticed. If priorities shift without explanation, it creates confusion. Great remote leaders are consistent in how they communicate, how they make decisions, and how they follow through. This consistency becomes a source of psychological safety. It tells the team, "You can rely on me." Trust and visibility are not mutually exclusive. They work together to complete each other. Visibility creates a shared context, whereas trust allows people to act freely within it. Together, they foster a culture of ownership in which people feel empowered to take the initiative, raise issues early, and deliver results without being micromanaged.

Emotional Presence: Leading with Empathy and Humanity

Remote leadership is more than just driving performance; it is also about nurturing people. When your team is dispersed, you lose the subtle cues of in-person interaction: tiredness after a long sprint, excitement after a breakthrough, and hesitation in a hallway conversation. This is why emotional presence is more important than ever. A great remote leader does more than just show up for work; they show up for their team.

Empathy is not optional in remote leadership; it is required. Without it, distance quickly becomes isolation. People start to feel invisible, disconnected, and unsupported. The most effective leaders prioritize asking how people are doing rather than what they are doing. They provide regular opportunities for human connection, whether through one-on-one check-ins, informal team hangouts, or simply a moment of genuine conversation during a team call. These check-ins are not about productivity but about people. They're a chance to listen deeply, notice patterns, and offer support. A team member who seems disengaged might be struggling with burnout. Another person who's missing deadlines might be facing challenges at home. Without emotional presence, these signals go unnoticed until it's too late. With it, leaders can respond early with compassion, adjustments, and encouragement.

Remote leaders also model vulnerability. They are honest about their own challenges, uncertainties, and learnings. This honesty builds trust and lowers the pressure for perfection. When people feel safe to speak openly, they're more likely to ask for help, admit mistakes, and collaborate meaningfully. Emotional presence also includes advocating for team well-being. That means respecting boundaries, discouraging "always-on" culture, and promoting rest as a legitimate part of high performance. It means protecting time for deep work, setting clear expectations around availability, and reinforcing that responsiveness does not equal productivity. Leaders who do this create teams that are not only high-performing but also sustainable.

And finally, great remote leaders build rituals of connection. These might be as simple as celebrating wins at the end of each week, recognizing birthdays, or sharing personal updates during meetings. These small moments, though not directly tied to output, are vital. They remind everyone that behind the code, tasks, and tickets, there are people who want to be seen, valued, and part of something meaningful.

Final Thoughts: The Human Core of Remote Leadership

Remote leadership is not about managing through distance; it's about connecting through intention. It's about creating relationships based on trust and concern, systems that promote transparency, and structures that allow autonomy. The most effective remote leaders are aware that their role is to empower each person, not to manage every little detail.

They don't teach; they lead by influence. Not through monitoring, but through consistency. Through presence, not pressure. In the absence of walls and desks, the most powerful tools a leader has are clarity, trust, and empathy. With them, even the most distributed team can feel close, aligned, and committed to a shared purpose. Leadership in remote work isn't just possible; it's a chance to redefine what leadership truly means.

Chapter Six

Building and Maintaining Team Culture

Company culture isn't confined to office walls, and it doesn't vanish when teams go remote, it simply transforms. In traditional co-located workplaces, culture is often absorbed passively. It's felt in the layout of the office, the energy of casual hallway conversations, the rhythm of shared lunches, and the ease of spontaneous social rituals. These subtle, ambient elements give team members a sense of shared identity, belonging, and purpose. In distributed teams, however, culture doesn't passively emerge; it must be intentionally designed. With no office environment to reinforce values or foster organic connection, remote culture becomes visible through tone, communication habits, inclusivity, and the ways in which people support one another across distance. It's built through systems, rituals, and, most importantly, consistent human behavior.

Strong remote culture doesn't come from perks or programs; it grows from values in action. It's not about offering virtual yoga or sending branded swag; it's about the daily moments where kindness is practiced, contributions are acknowledged, voices are heard, and trust is extended. In this environment, culture isn't accidental; it's constructed, practiced, and refined through repetition.

Culture by Design, Not by Default

In co-located teams, culture often forms unconsciously. Leaders and team members absorb it through observing how leaders make decisions, how colleagues treat one another, what behaviors are praised, and which ones are quietly tolerated. In remote teams, this passive absorption vanishes. Without physical proximity, culture becomes less visible and less easily transmitted. That doesn't mean it disappears; it simply becomes a matter of conscious design.

Culture in a remote setting shows up in the smallest of actions: how people communicate, how feedback is given, how conflict is resolved, and how people respond when things go wrong. When culture is neglected, remote work can begin to feel cold, transactional, and isolating. But when nurtured, it creates a deep sense of connection and psychological safety even between people who have never met in person. Leaders in remote teams have an outsized impact on shaping this environment. Not through mission statements or corporate slides, but through their own consistent actions. When leaders model transparency, kindness, humility, and inclusion, those values begin to permeate the team. When they acknowledge contributions, admit mistakes, and support learning, they set a tone that others follow. This influence is especially powerful in distributed settings, where ambiguity can breed disengagement if not countered by steady signals of care and clarity. One powerful tool for building intentional culture is documentation. Writing down core team values, communication norms, decision-making processes, and expectations around behavior helps everyone align. A documented code of conduct or "team charter" makes implicit expectations explicit, which is especially critical for teams operating across different cultures, time zones, and work styles. When expectations are clear, people are freer to bring their full selves to work, knowing they understand the rules of engagement.

The culture you design should also reflect the specific strengths of remote work: autonomy, flexibility, and deep focus. Instead of trying to mimic the in-office experience, strong remote cultures leverage the opportunity to work in asynchronous cycles, honor different time zones, and create thoughtful workflows that support both individual productivity and collective connection.

Fostering Inclusion Across Distance

Diversity may come naturally in distributed teams, but inclusion does not. With team members spread across regions, time zones, and cultural backgrounds, remote teams are often more demographically varied than traditional offices. But diversity alone isn't enough. Without intentional inclusion, those differences can turn into sources of disconnection or even exclusion.

Inclusion in remote teams starts with accessibility, ensuring everyone has a fair opportunity to participate. That includes being mindful of how meetings are scheduled, how decisions are made, and how input is gathered. If all meetings are held at times convenient to one time zone, or if only the most vocal participants are heard, teams risk leaving valuable perspectives out of the conversation. To address this, inclusive remote teams rotate meeting times or supplement meetings with asynchronous tools recorded videos, detailed notes, shared docs, or Loom updates. This ensures that participation isn't restricted to those who are awake and online during a specific window. It also gives introverted team members or non-native speakers a chance to process and respond thoughtfully, rather than being pressured to contribute on the spot. Beyond timing and logistics, inclusion requires leaders to recognize and adapt to different communication styles. Some team members may be hesitant to speak up in group calls but may offer deep insights when invited to contribute to writing. Others may need more context before offering ideas. Creating space for these differences and removing stigma around them is essential. It reinforces the message that there is no "one right way" to contribute, only shared goals and varied paths toward reaching them.

Inclusivity also involves recognizing and respecting individual needs and boundaries. In remote work, people often bring their full lives to the screen children, pets, caregiving responsibilities, or simply different rhythms and preferences. A team member may need to step away for an hour in the middle of the day or prefer deep work blocks with minimal Slack interruptions. Rather than seeing these differences as obstacles, inclusive teams treat them as realities to be supported. The strongest teams also create space for quieter voices and underrepresented perspectives. They encourage managers to check in privately with team members who may not feel comfortable raising issues in a group setting. They establish norms that allow people to challenge decisions respectfully and raise concerns without fear of judgment. Psychological safety, the belief that one can speak up without punishment or humiliation, is a cornerstone of inclusion. And in remote teams, it must be explicitly nurtured.

Celebrating Humanity, Not Just Productivity

Remote teams run the risk of becoming purely task oriented. With fewer casual conversations and minimal spontaneous interactions, it's easy for work to devolve into a sequence of checklists, updates, and deadlines. While this may seem efficient in the short term, over time it erodes morale, creativity, and connection. That's why great remote cultures go beyond productivity and actively celebrate humanity. They make space for joy, personality, humor, and informal connection, those vital ingredients that help teams bond and perform at their best. Celebrating achievements also plays a crucial role. In the absence of hallway high-fives or team lunches, leaders need to intentionally highlight wins big or small. That might be acknowledging a team member's great debugging session, sharing praise from a client, or simply thanking someone for helping onboard a new hire. Recognition, when done regularly and genuinely, fosters a culture of appreciation and pride.

Milestones like work anniversaries, birthdays, or project completions are also powerful culture touchpoints. They remind team members that they are valued not just for their output, but for their presence and contribution to the group. A quick message, a shared GIF, or a celebratory email can have an outsized emotional impact when thoughtfully delivered. Importantly, celebrating humanity also means creating space for emotional honesty. Remote leaders who check in on how people are feeling, not just what they're doing, foster deeper trust and connection. When people feel safe to say, "I'm overwhelmed," or "I'm feeling isolated," the team can respond with support and flexibility. These are the moments when culture is most powerfully expressed not in the absence of struggle, but in how a team shows up for one another during it.

In a healthy remote culture, performance and empathy are not at odds they fuel each other. People are more creative, collaborative, and resilient when they feel supported, seen, and respected. A culture that honors humanity builds teams that last. Remote work doesn't weaken culture it clarifies what truly creates it. When office walls fall away, what remains are the choices people make: how they communicate, how they collaborate, how they show respect, and how they build trust. Culture in remote teams is not accidental, it's deliberate. It is shaped by how leaders behave, how teams interact, and how inclusion is practiced every day. It is reinforced in Slack messages, video calls, code reviews, documentation, and decisions. It's built in micro-moments: a kind word, a thoughtful question, a note of appreciation, a space made for someone's voice. Strong remote cultures thrive on clarity, inclusion, and emotional presence. They value both performance and personhood. They understand that culture is not about mimicry; it's about meaning. When people choose to show up for one another with kindness, consistency, and curiosity, culture flourishes even across thousands of miles. Design your culture. Write it down. Live it daily. Because in remote teams, culture isn't where you are, it's how you are, together.

Chapter Seven

Agile in a Distributed Setting

When Agile methodology first emerged in the early 2000s, it was born from the energy of collocated teams developers huddled around whiteboards, product managers sketching user stories on sticky notes, and daily standups happening in crowded conference rooms. The original Agile Manifesto emphasized "individuals and interactions over processes and tools" and "customer collaboration over contract negotiation," principles that seemed inextricably linked to physical proximity and face-to-face communication. Yet as the global workforce has undergone a fundamental transformation toward remote and distributed work, a remarkable evolution has occurred. Teams scattered across continents and time zones have discovered that Agile's core philosophy not only survives in virtual environments but can actually flourish when properly adapted. The key insight is understanding that Agile is fundamentally a mindset a philosophy of iterative improvement, rapid feedback, and team empowerment rather than a rigid set of ceremonies tied to physical spaces. The transition from traditional, collocated Agile to distributed Agile requires more than simply moving standup meetings to video calls. It demands a fundamental reimagining of how teams collaborate, communicate, and maintain the rapid feedback loops that make Agile so powerful. This evolution challenges teams to preserve the spirit of Agile while adapting its practices to the realities of modern, distributed work.

Transforming Agile Practices for Distributed Teams

The most profound shift in remote Agile implementation lies in embracing asynchronous workflows while maintaining the collaborative spirit that makes Agile effective. Traditional Agile practices were designed around synchronous interactions: daily standups at 9 AM, sprint planning sessions where everyone gathered in the same room, and retrospectives conducted with the entire team present. In a distributed environment, these practices must evolve to accommodate different time zones, work schedules, and communication preferences. Asynchronous standups represent one of the most successful adaptations of traditional Agile ceremonies. Instead of requiring team members across multiple time zones to join a live meeting, teams can maintain momentum through written updates, voice recordings, or short video messages. These async updates often provide a richer context than traditional verbal standups, as team members have time to reflect on their progress, articulate blockers clearly, and provide thoughtful input on team priorities. The key to successful asynchronous Agile lies in creating structured communication channels that replace the organic information flow of collocated teams. Shared task boards become the central nervous system of the team, providing real-time visibility into progress, blockers, and upcoming work. Tools like automated check-ins, sprint dashboards, and integration-rich project management platforms ensure that information flows seamlessly without requiring constant meetings.

However, asynchronous work doesn't mean eliminating live interaction entirely. The most successful remote Agile teams use synchronous meetings strategically for sprint planning sessions that require collaborative decision-making, retrospectives that benefit from real-time discussion, and pair programming sessions where immediate feedback accelerates problem-solving. The difference is that these live interactions are purposeful and balanced with deep work time, allowing team members to maintain focus while staying connected to team goals. Sprint planning in distributed teams often becomes more thorough and inclusive than traditional collocated sessions. When teams can't rely on hallway conversations to clarify requirements, they invest more time in creating detailed user stories, acceptance criteria, and task breakdowns. This increased documentation, while requiring more upfront effort, often leads to clearer expectations and fewer mid-sprint surprises. Retrospectives, too, take on new dimensions in remote environments. Some teams conduct live retrospectives using digital collaboration tools, while others use asynchronous formats that allow team members to contribute thoughtfully over several days. The asynchronous approach often encourages more honest feedback, as team members have time to reflect on their experiences without the pressure of immediate response.

Building Visibility and Accountability in Virtual Environments

One of the greatest challenges in remote Agile implementation is replacing the natural awareness that comes from physical proximity. In collocated teams, progress is often visible at a glance you can see who's pair programming, which features are being tested, and when someone is stuck on a problem. In distributed teams, this organic visibility must be intentionally constructed through transparent systems and clear communication protocols. Project management tools become far more than simple task trackers in remote Agile environments; they become the primary interface for team awareness and coordination. Platforms like Jira, Linear, Trello, or ClickUp must provide not just task management but rich context about work progress, dependencies, and team capacity. The goal isn't micromanagement but rather creating a shared understanding of team priorities and progress. Effective remote Agile teams invest heavily in maintaining clean, well-organized backlogs with detailed user stories and clear acceptance criteria. When team members can't walk over to a product manager's desk for clarification, every story must be self-contained and comprehensive. This discipline in story writing often leads to better requirements gathering and fewer scope creep issues than traditional collocated approaches.

Documentation takes on increased importance in distributed Agile teams, but it must be living documentation rather than static artifacts. Decision logs, architectural diagrams, and process documentation become essential references that team members can access independently. The key is creating documentation that serves the team's immediate needs rather than satisfying abstract documentation requirements.

Regular grooming sessions become more critical in remote environments, as they provide structured opportunities to clarify requirements, estimate effort, and identify dependencies. These sessions often involve more detailed technical discussions than their collocated counterparts, as team members need to thoroughly understand requirements before diving into implementation. Code reviews and testing processes also require more structured approaches in remote environments. Without the ability to easily call someone over to look at code, teams must establish clear review protocols, comprehensive testing strategies, and well-defined deployment procedures. This increased structure often leads to higher code quality and more reliable releases.

The concept of "definition of done" becomes even more important in remote Agile teams. Clear criteria for when work is complete, tested, and ready for deployment eliminate ambiguity and ensure that all team members understand quality standards. This shared understanding is crucial when team members are working independently across different time zones.

Cultivating Remote Team Autonomy and Continuous Improvement

The most successful remote Agile teams embrace autonomy as a core principle, recognizing that distributed work requires team members to make decisions independently while maintaining alignment with team goals. This autonomy isn't about isolation or lack of coordination; rather, it's about empowering team members to execute effectively within clearly defined parameters. Autonomous remote teams require exceptionally clear product roadmaps and sprint goals. When developers can't easily seek clarification from product managers or stakeholders, they need comprehensive context about user needs, business priorities, and technical constraints. This clarity enables team members to make smart decisions about implementation details, technical trade-offs, and scopc adjustments without constant consultation. Communication protocols have become an essential infrastructure for autonomous remote teams. Establishing clear expectations about response times, communication channels, and escalation procedures ensures that team members can work independently while maintaining connection to the broader team. Some teams use "communication agreements" that specify when to use chat versus email, how quickly to respond to different types of messages, and when to escalate issues to synchronous discussion. Pair programming takes on new significance in remote environments, serving not just as a development practice but as a key mechanism for knowledge sharing and team bonding. While remote pair programming requires more intentional coordination than in-person collaboration, it often leads to more focused sessions and better documentation of decisions made during pairing.

Team building and relationship development require deliberate attention in remote Agile environments. Without casual hallway conversations and shared lunches, teams must create intentional opportunities for connection. Some teams hold virtual coffee chats, others organize online game sessions, and many invest in periodic in-person gatherings when possible. These relationship-building activities aren't just nice-to-haves; they're essential for maintaining the trust and communication that make Agile teams effective. Retrospectives become the cornerstone of continuous improvement in remote Agile teams. Without the organic feedback loops that occur naturally in collocated environments, retrospectives provide essential opportunities for reflection, adjustment, and evolution. The most effective remote retrospectives create safe spaces for honest feedback, focus on actionable improvements, and follow through on commitments made during the session. The feedback loop in remote retrospectives often extends beyond the traditional meeting format. Some teams use anonymous feedback tools, others create ongoing channels for process improvement suggestions, and many implement regular pulse surveys to gauge team satisfaction and identify emerging issues. The key is creating multiple avenues for feedback and ensuring that input leads to meaningful change.

Remote Agile teams must also be more intentional about celebrating successes and acknowledging contributions. Without the natural recognition that comes from shared physical presence, teams need to create explicit practices for celebrating milestones, recognizing individual contributions, and maintaining team morale. This might include virtual demo days, team newsletters highlighting accomplishments, or structured appreciation practices during retrospectives. The evolution of Agile for remote work represents more than just an adaptation to changing work patterns; it's a refinement of Agile principles that often leads to more disciplined, thoughtful, and effective practices. While remote Agile requires more intentional structure and communication, it can also enable deeper focus, more inclusive participation, and more sustainable work practices. The teams that successfully navigate this evolution often find that they've not only maintained the benefits of Agile but have discovered new ways to collaborate, innovate, and deliver value in an increasingly distributed world.

Chapter Eight

Remote Onboarding and Mentorship

The transition to remote work has fundamentally transformed how organizations build and maintain their teams. While the benefits of distributed work are well-documented increased flexibility, access to global talent, and reduced overhead costs the challenges of integrating new team members have become significantly more complex. Joining a new team has always been a vulnerable experience, filled with uncertainty about expectations, culture, and one's place within the organization. However, in remote settings, this vulnerability is amplified by the absence of traditional social cues and informal learning opportunities that naturally occur in physical workspaces. Without the benefit of office tours, spontaneous desk-side introductions, or casual lunchroom conversations, new remote employees often find themselves navigating their first days in what feels like a digital void. The simple act of logging into a remote team environment for the first time can feel like walking into a silent room with no clear understanding of where to stand, how to behave, or who to approach for guidance. This disorientation isn't merely uncomfortable, it can be professionally damaging, leading to slower productivity, decreased engagement, and ultimately, higher turnover rates.

In this context, onboarding and mentorship transcend their traditional roles as supportive practices and become mission-critical components of remote team success. When these systems are thoughtfully designed and consistently implemented, they provide new team members with far more than procedural knowledge. They deliver confidence, clear direction, and most importantly, a genuine sense of belonging within the organization. In remote environments, where the risk of isolation and disengagement is inherently higher, this foundation can literally determine whether someone thrives in their new role or quietly fades into disconnection. For remote organizations serious about building strong, sustainable teams, onboarding and mentorship must be treated as core infrastructure rather than optional add-ons. They represent the digital equivalent of a welcoming physical workspace, the difference between a new hire feeling like they've joined a cohesive team versus feeling like they're working in isolation with a group of strangers.

Creating Experiential Onboarding: Beyond Administrative Tasks

The most common mistake organizations make when approaching remote onboarding is treating it as a purely administrative exercise. The traditional checklist approach provision the laptop, set up system accounts, send the employee handbook, introduce the team via email fundamentally misunderstands what new hires actually need to succeed in a remote environment. While these administrative tasks are necessary, they represent only the most basic layer of integration. True onboarding in remote teams must be experiential, immersive, and deeply human. A comprehensive remote onboarding program serves as a guided journey through the team's values, tools, workflows, and cultural expectations. It anticipates the confusion that naturally arises when someone enters a new digital environment and proactively addresses the isolation that can emerge during those critical first days. This process begins well before the official start date. A thoughtful welcome email, complete with a detailed agenda for the first week and early access to essential tools, can significantly reduce pre-start anxiety while building genuine excitement about joining the team.

The first day itself requires careful orchestration. Rather than leaving new hires to navigate their initial login experiences alone, someone should be prepared to provide a warm, human welcome not through a generic tutorial or automated system, but through genuine personal interaction. This might involve a video call to walk through the digital workspace, a virtual coffee chat to discuss initial impressions, or a guided tour of the team's communication channels and collaboration tools. The first week should strategically balance self-paced learning with guided experiences and meaningful one-on-one interactions with key team members. Self-paced elements might include comprehensive documentation review, training modules, and familiarization with company tools and processes. Guided experiences could involve shadowing senior team members during meetings, participating in collaborative work sessions, or attending team ceremonies like sprint planning or retrospectives. One-on-one meetings should extend beyond immediate supervisors to include peers, cross-functional partners, and other stakeholders who can provide different perspectives on the role and organization.

Crucially, the first week should create numerous opportunities for new hires to observe how the team naturally communicates, approaches problem-solving, and makes decisions. This observational learning is particularly important in remote settings, where the subtle cues that help people understand team dynamics in physical offices are absent. New team members need to see how conflict is resolved, how feedback is given and received, how celebrations are conducted, and how the team maintains its culture across digital channels.

The buddy system represents one of the most powerful tools in remote onboarding. A buddy differs fundamentally from a manager or HR representative. They're a peer who's embedded within the team and can guide new hires through the real-world nuances of the work environment. Buddies answer the practical questions that often don't make it into formal documentation: What's the appropriate tone for chat messages? Where do we document design decisions? How do we celebrate team wins? Which meetings are truly optional versus culturally expected? Having a designated buddy removes the natural hesitation that comes with asking questions in a new environment. It provides new hires with an immediate connection point someone they can approach without feeling like they're interrupting important work or bothering busy colleagues. When properly structured, a buddy system becomes the crucial bridge between formal training and genuine belonging. It offers emotional support during vulnerable moments, provides technical guidance when systems inevitably confuse, and delivers cultural cues that help new team members navigate unwritten rules and expectations. The most effective buddy relationships are characterized by regular check-ins, clear expectations about availability and scope, and explicit encouragement to ask questions freely. Buddies should be chosen not just for their technical competence, but for their ability to communicate clearly, their patience with repetitive questions, and their genuine enthusiasm for helping others succeed.

Mentorship as Long-Term Growth Infrastructure

While buddy systems excel at short-term integration, mentorship addresses the longer-term challenge of professional development and sustained engagement in remote environments. In distributed teams, where it's remarkably easy to become isolated within individual work silos, mentorship becomes a powerful mechanism for maintaining connection, facilitating professional growth, and helping team members navigate complex challenges over time.

A mentor provides far more than technical advice or procedural guidance. They offer context about organizational history and decision-making processes, encouragement during difficult periods, and perspective that comes from having navigated similar challenges. In remote settings, where informal learning opportunities are limited, mentors become crucial sources of institutional knowledge and cultural understanding. Remote mentorship doesn't require elaborate formal structures or rigid meeting schedules. It might manifest as recurring virtual coffee chats, ongoing Slack threads for questions and discussions, shared documents containing resources and reflections, or periodic video calls to discuss career development. The key ingredient is consistency rather than formality. When someone knows there's a trusted person they can reach out to a guide who has been where they are and successfully navigated similar challenges, it strengthens both their professional skills and their emotional connection to the team.

Mentorship also serves as a crucial mechanism for culture transmission. Mentors model how the team communicates during stressful periods, how they handle setbacks and failures, and how they share successes and celebrate achievements. They pass down organizational values through their actions as much as their words, helping maintain cultural continuity even as teams grow, change, or face external pressures. The most effective mentorship relationships in remote environments are characterized by mutual respect, clear communication about expectations and boundaries, and genuine investment in the mentee's long-term success. Mentors should be chosen not just for their seniority or technical expertise, but for their ability to provide emotional support, their willingness to share honest feedback, and their commitment to helping others develop their careers. Organizations can support these relationships by providing mentorship training, creating structured frameworks for goal setting and progress tracking, and recognizing mentorship contributions as valuable work that deserves time and attention. Regular check-ins between mentors and mentees should focus not just on immediate work challenges but on longer-term career development, skill building, and professional satisfaction.

The Strategic Impact of Comprehensive Onboarding

The consequences of neglecting proper onboarding in remote teams extend far beyond individual discomfort or confusion. Poor onboarding creates a cascade of negative effects that can damage team performance, organizational culture, and business outcomes. Without adequate guidance and support, new hires inevitably flounder during their crucial first weeks. They miss important contextual information that would help them make better decisions, duplicate work that others have already completed or withdraw from team participation because they feel unprepared or unwelcome. In traditional office environments, small social cues and informal interactions often help new employees feel included and gradually build their confidence. A smile in the hallway, an invitation to join a lunch conversation, or overhearing how colleagues interact can all contribute to a sense of belonging. Remote environments lack these natural integration mechanisms, making new hires more likely to internalize silence as indifference or interpret minimal communication as rejection.

This dynamic leads to disengagement, slower productivity ramp-up, and in many cases, early turnover that could have been prevented with better onboarding. Organizations that fail to invest adequately in onboarding pay significant costs later through rehiring expenses, retraining investments, and lost momentum on important projects. The hidden costs include decreased team morale, reduced trust in leadership, and damage to the organization's reputation among potential future hires. Conversely, teams that prioritize comprehensive onboarding and ongoing mentorship consistently see stronger retention rates, faster productivity development, and deeper organizational commitment. New hires who experience thoughtful onboarding are more likely to become engaged contributors, cultural ambassadors, and long-term team members who help maintain the positive cycle by supporting future new hires.

The onboarding experience also sends a powerful signal about organizational values and priorities. A thoughtful, human-centered onboarding process communicates clearly: "We value your time and contribution. We genuinely want you here. We're committed to investing in your success." This message resonates far beyond the first week or month, becoming the foundation for trust, belonging, and loyalty that can sustain employee engagement through challenging periods. In distributed teams, where colleagues may never meet in person, the onboarding experience often represents the most intensive and personal interaction new hires will have with their team. If this first experience is welcoming, clear, and genuinely supportive, it establishes a foundation of positive relationships that can sustain remote collaboration for years. It transforms what might otherwise be a series of virtual handshakes into something meaningful and lasting the beginning of real professional relationships built on mutual respect and shared commitment to success. The investment in comprehensive onboarding and mentorship isn't just about individual success; it's about building the kind of remote team culture that can attract top talent, maintain high performance, and adapt successfully to future challenges. In an increasingly distributed work environment, organizations that master these fundamentals will have significant competitive advantages in building and maintaining exceptional teams.

Chapter Nine

Conflict, Feedback, and Difficult Conversations

Remote work has fundamentally transformed how teams collaborate, communicate, and occasionally clash. While the digital workspace offers unprecedented flexibility and global connectivity, it also presents unique challenges that can amplify interpersonal tensions and create new sources of conflict. The absence of spontaneous hallway conversations, the nuanced loss of body language, and the persistent hum of asynchronous communication can transform minor misunderstandings into significant team disruptions. Yet conflict, when approached with intention and skill, becomes one of the most powerful catalysts for team growth and innovation. It illuminates blind spots that might otherwise remain hidden, challenges assumptions that limit creativity, and ultimately strengthens relationships when navigated with care and respect. The key distinction lies not in avoiding conflict, an impossible and counterproductive goal, but in developing sophisticated approaches to recognize, address, and learn from these inevitable tensions. In distributed teams, this navigation requires a fundamental shift in mindset and methodology. The casual check-ins that might defuse tension in a physical office don't exist in remote environments. The ability to read micro-expressions, gauge energy levels, or catch someone for a quick clarifying conversation disappears behind screens and time zones. Instead, remote teams must develop more intentional, structured, and empathetic approaches to conflict resolution that account for the unique dynamics of digital collaboration.

The stakes are particularly high in remote settings because unresolved conflicts can fester in isolation, growing more complex and emotionally charged over time. Without the natural pressure release valves of in-person interaction, team members may withdraw, become passive-aggressive, or allow frustrations to compound until they reach a breaking point. This makes proactive conflict management not just beneficial but essential for maintaining team cohesion and productivity.

Understanding and Addressing Conflict in Remote Environments

The anatomy of remote conflict differs significantly from its in-person counterpart, often beginning with seemingly innocuous digital interactions that spiral into larger tensions. A hastily written email sent between meetings may lack the warmth and context that would naturally accompany a face-to-face conversation. A delayed response to a urgent message might be interpreted as indifference or resistance when it's actually the result of overlapping schedules or technical difficulties. These misunderstandings accumulate like sediment, gradually building barriers between team members who might otherwise collaborate seamlessly. The digital medium itself contributes to these challenges through what researchers call "media richness theory" the idea that different communication channels carry varying amounts of information. Text-based communication, while efficient, strips away vocal tone, facial expressions, and the subtlc social cues that help us interpret intent and emotion. When someone writes "fine" in a chat message, the recipient must guess whether this indicates genuine agreement, reluctant acceptance, or barely contained frustration. This ambiguity creates space for projection and misinterpretation that can quickly escalate into more serious conflicts.

Time zone differences compound these communication challenges by creating natural delays in clarification and resolution. A misunderstanding that occurs at the end of one person's workday may not be addressed until the next day or even later, giving negative emotions time to intensify and assumptions to solidify. By the time the parties reconnect, what began as a simple miscommunication may have evolved into a more complex interpersonal issue requiring significant effort to untangle. Cultural differences, often more pronounced in globally distributed teams, add another layer of complexity to remote conflict. Communication styles that feel direct and efficient in one culture may seem harsh or dismissive in another. Decision-making processes that appear collaborative in some contexts might feel chaotic or inefficient to team members from cultures that value hierarchy and clear authority. These cultural misalignments can create persistent friction that affects team dynamics long after the initial incident.

Recognizing these unique characteristics of remote conflict is the foundation for developing effective responses. Teams must acknowledge that digital communication requires more explicit emotional intelligence, clearer expression of intent, and greater patience for clarification and understanding. This recognition should inform how team members craft their messages, interpret others' communications, and approach potential conflicts with curiosity rather than defensiveness. Creating structured pathways for addressing conflict becomes crucial in remote environments where spontaneous resolution is less likely. Teams should establish clear protocols for escalating concerns, whether through private video calls, dedicated channels for sensitive discussions, or mediated conversations with neutral facilitators. These pathways should be communicated clearly and reinforced regularly, ensuring that team members know how and when to raise concerns before they become larger problems. The importance of emotional regulation in remote conflict cannot be overstated. Without the natural social pressure and immediate feedback of in-person interaction, team members may need to develop stronger self-management skills to pause before responding, seek clarification before assuming negative intent, and approach conflicts with genuine curiosity about others' perspectives. This emotional intelligence becomes a core competency for remote team success, requiring ongoing development and practice. Prevention strategies play a particularly important role in remote conflict management.

Regular check-ins, clear communication protocols, and explicit discussion of working styles and preferences can help prevent many conflicts before they occur. Teams should invest time in understanding each member's communication preferences, work rhythms, and cultural backgrounds to create a foundation of mutual understanding that reduces the likelihood of misinterpretation.

Constructive Feedback and Difficult Conversations

The art of giving and receiving feedback transforms dramatically into remote environments, requiring a complete reimagining of how teams share perspectives, address concerns, and drive continuous improvement. Feedback, often called the currency of growth, becomes both more crucial and more challenging when filtered through digital channels. The absence of immediate visual and auditory cues means that feedback providers must be extraordinarily thoughtful about their approach, while recipients must develop new skills for interpreting and responding to input delivered through screens and text.

Effective remote feedback begins with timing and context. Unlike in-person feedback that can be delivered spontaneously in the moment, remote feedback requires more strategic planning. The feedback provider must consider not just what to say, but when to say it, through which channel, and how to create the right environment for productive discussion. A complex piece of feedback delivered through chat during a busy workday may be misunderstood or inadequately processed, while the same feedback delivered thoughtfully through video call with dedicated time for discussion can become a catalyst for meaningful growth. The structure of remote feedback requires particular attention to clarity and specificity. Vague feedback like "your presentation could be better" becomes especially problematic in remote settings where there's no opportunity for immediate clarification or follow-up questions. Instead, effective remote feedback follows a pattern of specific observation, impact description, and collaborative solution-finding. For example, "I noticed that the data visualization in slide seven was difficult to read during the screen share, which made it challenging for the team to engage with the key findings. Could we explore ways to make the charts more readable in our virtual format?"

The emotional dimension of feedback delivery requires heightened attention in remote environments. Without the ability to read body language and make real-time adjustments based on the recipient's reaction, feedback providers must be more intentional about creating psychological safety and demonstrating genuine care for the recipient's growth. This might involve starting with affirmation, explicitly stating positive intent, and creating multiple opportunities for the recipient to ask questions or share their perspective.

Written feedback, while offering the advantage of careful composition and permanent reference, requires particular finesse to avoid misinterpretation. The tone that seems constructive in the writer's mind may feel harsh or critical to the reader. Successful remote feedback writers develop sensitivity to how their words might be received, often reading their feedback aloud or asking colleagues to review sensitive messages before sending. They also learn to use qualifying language, offer multiple perspectives, and create space for dialogue rather than delivering pronouncements. Video-based feedback conversations require their own set of skills and considerations. The feedback provider must manage the technical aspects of the call while maintaining focus on the human connection and emotional dynamics. This includes being mindful of camera angles, lighting, and audio quality that might affect the recipient's comfort level, as well as creating a private, distraction-free environment that signals the importance of the conversation.

Difficult conversations in remote settings demand even greater care and intentionality. Performance concerns, interpersonal conflicts, or policy violations cannot be addressed through casual encounters or quick sidebar conversations. Instead, these conversations require formal scheduling, careful preparation, and structured approaches that ensure all parties feel heard and respected. The stakes are higher because the remote format offers fewer opportunities for repair and follow-up if the conversation goes poorly. The preparation phase for difficult remote conversations should include consideration of the recipient's perspective, anticipation of potential reactions, and development of specific, actionable outcomes. The conversation facilitator should prepare clear examples, relevant documentation, and potential solutions while also planning for how to manage their own emotions and responses during what may be a challenging discussion.

Opening difficult conversations in remote settings requires particular attention to setting the right tone and establishing psychological safety. This might involve acknowledging the challenge of having such conversations remotely, expressing genuine care for the relationship and the person's success, and clearly stating the constructive intent behind the discussion. The facilitator should also establish ground rules for the conversation, including agreements about confidentiality, how decisions will be made, and what follow-up actions will be taken.

The structure of difficult remote conversations should balance thorough discussion with clear progression toward resolution. This might involve starting with shared observations and experiences, moving through different perspectives on the situation, and culminating in collaborative problem-solving and concrete action steps. Throughout the conversation, the facilitator should check for understanding, create space for questions and clarifications, and ensure that all parties feel heard and respected.

Follow-up after difficult conversations becomes crucial in remote environments where there are fewer opportunities for casual check-ins and relationship repair. This might involve scheduled follow-up meetings, written summaries of agreements and action steps, and ongoing support for implementing changes. The goal is to ensure that difficult conversations lead to genuine resolution and improved relationships rather than temporary fixes that may deteriorate over time.

Building Resilient Feedback Cultures and Learning Systems

The transformation of occasional feedback into a thriving culture of continuous improvement represents one of the most significant challenges and opportunities for remote teams. Unlike traditional office environments where feedback culture can develop organically through daily interactions and observable behaviors, remote teams must be extraordinarily intentional about creating systems, norms, and practices that encourage regular, high-quality feedback exchanges. A resilient feedback culture in remote environments begins with leadership modeling and explicit value articulation. Team leaders must demonstrate vulnerability by seeking feedback on their own performance, acknowledging their mistakes openly, and showing genuine appreciation for input from team members. This modeling behavior sends powerful signals about the safety and value of feedback within the team. However, in remote settings, this modeling must be more visible and intentional than in traditional offices where leadership behavior is naturally observed throughout the day. The structural elements of remote feedback culture require careful design and consistent reinforcement. This might include regular retrospectives that go beyond project outcomes to examine communication patterns, relationship dynamics, and individual growth areas. "Feedback Fridays" or similar dedicated times for peer input can normalize the practice and reduce the emotional weight often associated with feedback conversations. Peer review rotations, where team members regularly provide input on each other's work, can distribute the feedback load and create multiple perspectives on individual performance.

Technology plays a crucial role in enabling sustainable feedback cultures for remote teams. Digital platforms can facilitate anonymous feedback when appropriate, create structured templates for regular input, and provide tracking systems that help ensure feedback leads to actionable change. However, the technology must be chosen and implemented thoughtfully to enhance rather than mechanize the fundamentally human process of growth and development.

The concept of psychological safety becomes paramount in remote feedback cultures, requiring explicit attention and ongoing cultivation. Team members must feel confident that expressing concerns, admitting mistakes, or providing challenging feedback won't result in punishment, exclusion, or retaliation. In remote environments, where social dynamics are less visible and relationships may feel more fragile, building this safety requires consistent effort and clear communication about team values and expectations. Effective remote feedback cultures also require diversity in feedback types and formats. Not all feedback needs to be formal or structured; teams should create space for appreciation, quick observations, and developmental suggestions. Some team members may prefer written feedback they can process privately, while others thrive on real-time verbal input. The culture should accommodate these differences while maintaining consistency in quality and constructiveness. The measurement and evolution of feedback culture presents unique challenges in remote environments. Traditional indicators like team morale surveys or observation of interpersonal dynamics may not capture the full picture of how feedback is being received and applied. Teams need to develop new metrics and assessment methods that account for the digital nature of their interactions while still providing meaningful insights into cultural health. Learning from conflict represents the ultimate expression of mature feedback culture, transforming potentially destructive tensions into opportunities for team growth and improved processes. This requires a fundamental shift in how teams view conflict from something to be avoided or quickly resolved to something that can provide valuable information about team dynamics, communication patterns, and systemic issues. The process of learning from conflict begins with systematic reflection and analysis. Teams should regularly examine not just what conflicts occurred, but what patterns emerge across different incidents. Are certain types of misunderstandings recurring? Do conflicts tend to escalate at particular times or around specific processes? Are there team members who consistently struggle with certain types of interactions? This analysis helps identify root causes rather than just addressing symptoms. Documentation and knowledge sharing become crucial elements of learning from conflict in remote environments. Unlike traditional offices where conflict resolution lessons might be shared through informal conversations or storytelling, remote teams must be more systematic about capturing and disseminating insights. This might involve creating shared repositories of conflict resolution strategies, developing case studies from past incidents, or establishing mentorship programs where experienced team members help others navigate challenging situations.

The integration of conflict learning into team development requires ongoing attention and commitment. Teams should regularly revisit their communication protocols, feedback practices, and conflict resolution procedures based on what they've learned from past incidents. This continuous improvement approach ensures that the team's capacity for handling conflict grows over time rather than remaining static.

Creating accountability for learning from conflict requires both individual and collective commitment. Team members should be encouraged to reflect on their own roles in conflicts and identify areas for personal growth, while the team as a whole should commit to implementing systemic changes that prevent similar issues from recurring. This dual focus on individual and collective responsibility creates a comprehensive approach to conflict learning. The ultimate goal of building resilient feedback cultures and learning systems is to create remote teams that are not just effective at avoiding conflict, but skilled at leveraging conflict for growth and innovation. These teams understand that tension and disagreement are natural parts of collaborative work, especially in the complex environment of remote collaboration. They develop sophisticated skills for navigating these challenges while maintaining strong relationships and high performance. Teams that successfully build these capabilities often find that their remote work experience becomes richer and more satisfying than traditional office-based collaboration. The intentionality required for effective remote conflict management creates deeper understanding between team members, more explicit communication practices, and stronger problem-solving capabilities that serve the team well across all aspects of their work. The investment in building these systems pays dividends not just in conflict resolution, but in overall team effectiveness and satisfaction.

Chapter Ten

Sustainability and Avoiding Burnout

The digital revolution has fundamentally transformed how we conceptualize work, workspace, and work-life integration. Remote work, once considered a fringe benefit or temporary accommodation, has evolved into a dominant force reshaping the global employment landscape. This transformation has been accelerated by technological advances, changing employee expectations, and global events that have forced organizations to reconsider traditional workplace models. However, as millions of professionals have discovered, the transition from office-based to remote work is not merely a change of location, it represents a fundamental reimagining of work culture, personal boundaries, and organizational structures. The initial euphoria of working from home, with its promise of flexibility, autonomy, and work-life balance, has given way to a more complex reality. For many, the dream of remote work has evolved into a nightmare of blurred boundaries, constant connectivity, and unprecedented levels of burnout.

Remote work has long been praised for its flexibility and freedom, but without careful structure and boundaries, that same freedom can become overwhelming. When your home becomes your office, and your laptop is always within reach, the lines between living and working blur dangerously. Days stretch longer, breaks become rare, and the expectation of being always available creeps in silently. Over time, this imbalance drains energy, dulls creativity, and eventually leads to burnout a condition that has reached epidemic proportions in the remote work era. The statistics paint a sobering picture. Studies conducted across various industries reveal that remote workers are experiencing higher rates of anxiety, depression, and burnout than their office-based counterparts. The very flexibility that makes remote work attractive has become a double-edged sword, cutting away at the natural boundaries that once protected workers from the endless demands of modern business.

Yet this challenge is not insurmountable. The key lies in understanding that sustainability in remote teams isn't about working less, it's about working smarter, with rhythm and recovery built into the process. It's about creating a culture that respects personal time, supports mental health, and empowers people to perform at their best without sacrificing their well-being. For distributed teams to thrive long-term, they must be designed not just for productivity, but for sustainable well-being. This comprehensive guide explores the multifaceted challenge of building sustainable remote teams. We will examine the structural, cultural, and individual elements that contribute to long-term success in distributed work environments. Through detailed analysis, practical strategies, and real-world examples, we will uncover how organizations can create remote work cultures that not only survive but thrive over the long term. The journey toward sustainable remote work requires a fundamental shift in how we think about productivity, success, and human well-being in professional contexts. It demands that we move beyond the traditional metrics of success hours worked, tasks completed, immediate availability toward a more holistic understanding of what it means to build effective, resilient teams in the digital age.

Understanding the Psychological Landscape of Remote Work

The transition to remote work represents more than a logistical change. It constitutes a psychological transformation that affects every aspect of how individuals relate to their work, their colleagues, and themselves. To build sustainable remote teams, we must first understand the complex psychological dynamics that emerge when work becomes untethered from traditional physical and temporal boundaries.

The human brain is remarkably adept at creating associations between physical spaces and mental states. For generations, the office has served as a psychological cue that signals the transition from personal to professional mindset. The commute, however tedious, provided a buffer zone a mental decompression chamber that allowed individuals to prepare for work and, equally importantly, to decompress afterward.

Remote work eliminates these natural transition points, creating a psychological environment where the boundaries between work and personal life become increasingly permeable. This permeability manifests in numerous ways. The bedroom becomes a conference room, the kitchen table transforms into a workspace, and the living room serves as a backdrop for video calls. Each of these spaces carries emotional and psychological associations that can either enhance or detract from work performance. More critically, the constant presence of work-related stimuli in personal spaces can create a state of chronic low-level stress, where the mind never fully disengages from work concerns.

The concept of "psychological safety" takes on new dimensions in remote work environments. While physical safety is generally assured in home environments, psychological safety the belief that one can speak up, make mistakes, and be vulnerable without fear of negative consequences becomes more complex to establish and maintain. The absence of non-verbal cues, the delay in communication, and the reduced opportunities for informal relationship building all contribute to a sense of psychological distance that can undermine team cohesion and individual confidence. Research in environmental psychology reveals that our physical surroundings profoundly influence our cognitive performance, creativity, and emotional well-being. The home environment, while familiar and comfortable, was not designed to optimize professional performance. Lighting, acoustics, ergonomics, and spatial organization all play crucial roles in cognitive function, yet most remote workers must improvise these elements within existing domestic spaces. The isolation inherent in remote work also triggers deep-seated human needs for connection and belonging. Humans are fundamentally social creatures, and the workplace has traditionally served as a primary source of social interaction and community. Remote work can lead to a phenomenon known as "social starvation," where the absence of casual conversations, shared meals, and collaborative energy creates a sense of professional loneliness that can significantly impact mental health and job satisfaction.

Understanding these psychological dynamics is crucial for leaders and team members alike. It provides the foundation for creating remote work environments that support rather than undermine human well-being. This understanding also helps explain why traditional productivity metrics may be inadequate for evaluating remote work success. They fail to account for the psychological costs and benefits that significantly impact long-term sustainability.

The Neuroscience of Remote Work and Cognitive Load

The shift to remote work has profound implications for cognitive function and brain health. Neuroscientific research reveals that remote work environments place unique demands on the brain, creating new forms of cognitive load that can either enhance or impair performance depending on how they are managed. Video conferencing, now a cornerstone of remote work, exemplifies these cognitive challenges. The phenomenon known as "Zoom fatigue" is not merely a colloquial term, it represents a genuine neurological burden.

During video calls, the brain must work harder to process non-verbal cues, manage audio delays, and maintain attention in an environment filled with digital distractions. The constant need to monitor one's own appearance while simultaneously focusing on others creates a form of cognitive dissonance that can be mentally exhausting.

The absence of peripheral vision in video calls also affects social cognition. In face-to-face interactions, we unconsciously process information from our peripheral vision, the body language of other participants, environmental cues, and subtle social dynamics. Video calls eliminate this peripheral information, forcing the brain to work harder to maintain social awareness and connection. Multitasking, while often celebrated as a productivity enhancement, becomes more problematic in remote work environments. The home setting provides numerous opportunities for task-switching from household chores to personal communications that can fragment attention and reduce cognitive efficiency. Neuroscientific research consistently demonstrates that multitasking reduces overall productivity and increases mental fatigue, effects that are amplified in remote work settings.

The concept of "attention residue" becomes particularly relevant in remote work environments. When we switch between tasks, a portion of our attention remains stuck on the previous task, creating a cumulative effect that can significantly impair cognitive performance. In traditional office environments, physical transitions between meetings and tasks provide natural opportunities for attention to fully shift. Remote work eliminates many of these natural transitions, creating a more continuous cognitive load. However, remote work also offers unique opportunities for cognitive optimization. The ability to control one's environment, eliminate office distractions, and align work with natural energy rhythms can enhance cognitive performance for many individuals. The key lies in understanding how to structure remote work environments to maximize these benefits while minimizing the cognitive costs.

Circadian rhythm research reveals that cognitive performance naturally fluctuates throughout the day, with most individuals experiencing peak performance in the mid-morning and experiencing a natural dip in the early afternoon. Remote work offers the opportunity to align work tasks with these natural rhythms, potentially enhancing overall productivity and well-being. Complex cognitive tasks can be scheduled during peak performance periods, while routine tasks can be relegated to periods of lower cognitive capacity. The role of physical movement in cognitive function cannot be overlooked. Traditional office environments, despite their limitations, naturally incorporate movement through walking to meetings, traveling between floors, and navigating office spaces. Remote work can become dangerously sedentary, depriving the brain of the cognitive benefits associated with physical activity. Research demonstrates that even brief periods of physical movement can enhance creativity, problem-solving, and overall cognitive function.

Sleep quality, crucial for cognitive performance and emotional regulation, can be both enhanced and compromised by remote work arrangements. The elimination of commuting time can allow for more sleep, but the presence of work-related stimuli in the bedroom can disrupt sleep quality. The blue light emitted by screens, particularly problematic when used in the evening, can disrupt circadian rhythms and compromise sleep quality.

Building Psychological Resilience in Distributed Teams

Psychological resilience the ability to bounce back from setbacks, adapt to change, and maintain well-being under stress becomes crucial for long-term success in remote work environments. Building resilience is not merely an individual responsibility; it requires systematic organizational support and cultural reinforcement.

The concept of "psychological flexibility" emerges as a key component of remote work resilience. This involves the ability to adapt one's behavior to changing circumstances, to tolerate uncertainty and ambiguity, and to maintain effectiveness despite challenges. Remote work environments are inherently more ambiguous than traditional office settings, requiring individuals to develop higher levels of psychological flexibility. Cognitive reframing techniques have become essential tools for remote workers. The ability to reinterpret challenges as opportunities, to view setbacks as learning experiences, and to maintain perspective during difficult periods can significantly impact long-term well-being and performance. Organizations can support this by providing training in cognitive reframing techniques and by modeling positive reframing in leadership communications. The development of "emotional granularity "the ability to distinguish between different emotional states and understand their causes becomes particularly important in remote work environments. Without the benefit of face-to-face interaction, remote workers must become more skilled at recognizing and articulating their emotional states. This enhanced emotional awareness can lead to better self-regulation and more effective communication with team members.

Building resilience also requires the development of robust social support networks. In traditional office environments, these networks often develop naturally through proximity and shared experiences. Remote work requires more intentional effort to build and maintain these relationships. Organizations can support this by creating structured opportunities for social interaction, facilitating mentor relationships, and encouraging informal communication channels.

The concept of "post-traumatic growth" becomes relevant for teams that have experienced significant challenges or setbacks. Rather than simply recovering from difficulties, resilient teams can use these experiences as opportunities for growth, learning, and improved performance. This requires a culture that views challenges as opportunities rather than threats, and that celebrates learning and adaptation over perfectionism. Stress inoculation training, borrowed from clinical psychology, can be adapted for remote work environments. This involves gradually exposing individuals to manageable levels of stress while providing them with coping strategies and support. Over time, this builds resilience and confidence in handling more significant challenges.

The role of meaning and purpose in building resilience cannot be overstated. Remote workers who have a clear understanding of how their work contributes to larger organizational goals and societal benefit demonstrate higher levels of resilience and job satisfaction. Organizations can support this by regularly communicating the impact of individual contributions and by connecting daily tasks to larger organizational missions.

Establishing Boundaries as a Foundation for Balance

The establishment of clear, sustainable boundaries represents one of the most critical challenges in remote work environments. Without the natural cues of an office environment the morning commute, the lunch break, the closing time remote workers must establish their own boundaries between work and personal life. This task, seemingly simple, requires significant psychological and practical effort. The idea of boundaries in remote work extends beyond simple time management. It encompasses physical boundaries (dedicated workspace), temporal boundaries (defined work hours), emotional boundaries (separation of work and personal emotions), and technological boundaries (appropriate use of work devices and platforms). Each of these dimensions requires careful consideration and intentional management.

Physical boundaries involve creating dedicated spaces for work that can be psychologically "closed off" when work ends. This doesn't necessarily require a separate office, it can be as simple as a specific area of a room that is used only for work, or even a portable setup that can be assembled and disassembled as needed. The key is creating a physical trigger that signals the transition between work and personal time. The psychology of physical boundaries is rooted in the concept of "environmental psychology", the study of how physical spaces affect human behavior and well-being. When work and personal spaces overlap completely, it becomes difficult for the brain to distinguish between work time and personal time, leading to chronic stress and difficulty "switching off" from work concerns.

Temporal boundaries require the establishment of clear start and end times for work activities. However, in remote work environments, these boundaries often become fluid due to the convenience of constant access to work materials and communications. The challenge is compounded by the fact that remote workers often feel pressure to demonstrate their productivity by being available outside of traditional work hours. The establishment of temporal boundaries requires both individual discipline and organizational support. Organizations must explicitly communicate expectations about work hours and availability, and they must model these expectations through leadership behavior. When managers send emails late at night or expect immediate responses to non-urgent communications, they inadvertently signal that boundaries are not respected or valued.

Emotional boundaries involve the ability to separate work-related emotions from personal well-being. In traditional office environments, physical separation provides a natural buffer that allows individuals to process and leave work-related stress at the office. Remote work eliminates this buffer, making it more likely that work-related stress will spill over into personal time and relationships. The development of emotional boundaries requires the cultivation of emotional intelligence and self-awareness. Remote workers must become skilled at recognizing when work-related emotions are affecting their personal well-being and develop strategies for managing these emotions effectively. This might involve end-of-day reflection practices, physical exercise, or other activities that help process and release work-related stress. Technological boundaries involve establishing appropriate limits on the use of work-related technology during personal time. The convenience of smartphones and laptops makes it easy to "quickly check" work emails or messages during personal time, but this constant connectivity can prevent the mental disengagement necessary for recovery and well-being. The establishment of technological boundaries requires both individual discipline and organizational policies. Some organizations have implemented "right to disconnect" policies that prohibit work-related communications outside of designated hours. Others have developed technological solutions that automatically delay the delivery of non-urgent messages until work hours.

The challenge of boundary establishment is complicated by the fact that remote work often provides genuine flexibility that can benefit both individuals and organizations. The key is finding the right balance between flexibility and boundaries maintaining enough structure to protect well-being while preserving the benefits of remote work flexibility.

The Role of Leadership in Modeling Sustainable Practices

Leadership plays a crucial role in establishing and maintaining sustainable remote work cultures. The behavior of leaders sends powerful signals about organizational values and expectations, and these signals are often more influential than formal policies or procedures. In remote work environments, where informal observation and social cues are reduced, leadership modeling becomes even more critical. Effective remote leadership requires a fundamental shift from traditional command-and-control models to more collaborative, trust-based approaches. The inability to directly observe employee activity forces leaders to focus on outcomes rather than processes, requiring a higher level of trust and a different set of management skill. Servant leadership " becomes particularly relevant in remote work environments. This leadership philosophy emphasizes the leader's role as a facilitator and supporter rather than a director. Remote leaders must become skilled at identifying and removing obstacles, providing resources and support, and creating conditions for team success rather than micromanaging daily activities.

Transparency in communication becomes crucial for remote leadership. In traditional office environments, leaders can rely on informal interactions, body language, and environmental cues to communicate information and maintain relationships. Remote leadership requires more intentional and explicit communication about expectations, priorities, and organizational changes. The modeling of work-life balance by leaders is particularly important in remote work environments. When leaders consistently work outside of normal hours, respond to emails immediately, or cancel personal commitments for work, they send a message that these behaviors are expected and valued. Conversely, when leaders demonstrate respect for boundaries, take time off, and prioritize well-being, they give permission for others to do the same.

Remote leaders must also become skilled at recognizing signs of burnout and overwhelm in team members. Without the benefit of visual cues and informal interactions, these signs can be more subtle and harder to detect. This requires developing new skills in virtual communication, regular check-ins, and creating safe spaces for team members to express concerns.

The concept of "psychological safety" becomes particularly important in remote work environments. Team members must feel safe to express concerns, admit mistakes, and ask for help without fear of negative consequences. Creating psychological safety requires intentional effort from leaders, including modeling vulnerability, responding positively to concerns, and creating structured opportunities for feedback and discussion. Effective remote leadership also requires the ability to create a sense of shared purpose and connection among team members. In traditional office environments, shared experiences and informal interactions naturally build team cohesion. Remote leaders must create intentional opportunities for team building, shared experiences, and informal interaction. The development of other leaders within the team becomes crucial for sustainable remote work. Rather than centralizing all leadership responsibilities, effective remote leaders distribute leadership functions among team members, creating a more resilient and adaptable team structure. This distributed leadership model also helps prevent leader burnout and creates more opportunities for team member growth and development.

Creating Flexible Schedules That Serve People

One of the most significant advantages of remote work is the potential for flexible scheduling that aligns with individual needs, preferences, and life circumstances. However, flexibility must be thoughtfully implemented to avoid becoming a source of stress and confusion rather than a benefit. The concept of "chronotype" individual differences in circadian rhythms and energy patterns becomes crucial for understanding how to implement effective flexible scheduling. Some individuals are naturally most alert and productive in the early morning, while others peak in the evening. Traditional office schedules often fail to accommodate these natural variations, leading to reduced productivity and well-being.

Flexible scheduling in remote work environments can allow individuals to align their work with their natural energy patterns, potentially enhancing both productivity and job satisfaction. However, this requires careful coordination to ensure that team collaboration and communication are not compromised. The implementation of flexible scheduling requires clear communication about core collaboration hours when team members are expected to be available for meetings and real-time communication. Outside of these core hours, individuals can structure their work according to their personal preferences and life circumstances. "time sovereignty" emerges as a key benefit of flexible remote work scheduling. This involves giving individuals greater control over how they structure their time, allowing them to integrate work and personal responsibilities in ways that work best for their individual circumstances. This might involve working early in the morning and taking afternoon breaks for personal activities or working intensively for several days and taking longer breaks.

However, flexible scheduling also requires strong self-management skills and clear communication about availability and deadlines. Not all individuals thrive with high levels of scheduling flexibility, and some may prefer more structured arrangements. The key is providing options and support for different working styles and preferences. The challenge of coordinating across time zones becomes more complex with flexible scheduling. Teams that include members in different time zones must be particularly thoughtful about scheduling meetings and coordinating work activities. This often requires a more asynchronous approach to work, with greater emphasis on written communication and documentation.

Flexible scheduling can also create challenges for work-life balance if not properly managed. The ability to work at any time can lead to the temptation to work all the time, particularly for individuals who struggle with boundary setting. Organizations must provide clear guidance and support for managing flexible schedules in ways that support rather than undermine well-being.

Building Team Cohesion Across Distance

The development of strong team cohesion represents one of the most significant challenges in remote work environments. Without the benefit of physical proximity, shared experiences, and informal interactions, remote teams must work harder to develop the trust, communication, and mutual support that characterize high-performing teams.

The concept of "swift trust" becomes crucial for remote team effectiveness. Unlike traditional teams that have time to develop trust gradually through repeated interactions, remote teams often need to develop trust quickly to function effectively. This requires more intentional effort to establish credibility, demonstrate reliability, and communicate openly about capabilities and limitations. The development of team cohesion requires intentional investment in relationship building. This involves creating opportunities for team members to get to know each other as individuals, not just as professional colleagues. Virtual coffee chats, online team-building activities, and informal communication channels can help build these relationships. Social presence can be enhanced through regular video communication, personal sharing, and attention to the relational aspects of team interactions.

Shared experiences play a crucial role in building team cohesion. In traditional office environments, these shared experiences occur naturally through daily interactions, shared challenges, and informal conversations. Remote teams must create intentional opportunities for shared experiences, such as virtual team events, collaborative projects, and shared learning opportunities. The development of team rituals and traditions can help create a sense of identity and belonging in remote teams. These might include regular team meetings with personal check-ins, celebration of achievements, or shared participation in online activities. The key is creating consistent, meaningful experiences that reinforce team identity and connection. Communication patterns significantly impact team cohesion in remote environments. Teams that communicate frequently, openly, and inclusively tend to develop stronger cohesion than those that communicate primarily through formal channels. This requires attention to both the frequency and quality of team communication. Creating psychological safety requires intentional effort from team leaders and members to respond positively to vulnerability and to create inclusive communication patterns. Conflict resolution becomes more challenging in remote teams due to the absence of non-verbal cues and the potential for misunderstandings in written communication. Remote teams must develop stronger conflict resolution skills and create clear processes for addressing disagreements and tensions when they arise. The celebration of achievements and milestones becomes particularly important for remote team cohesion. Without the informal recognition that occurs naturally in office environments, remote teams must create intentional opportunities to acknowledge accomplishments and celebrate successes.

The economic implications of sustainable remote work extend far beyond simple cost savings from reduced office space. A comprehensive economic analysis reveals that sustainable remote work practices can create significant value for organizations while also providing economic benefits for employees and society as a whole. From an organizational perspective, sustainable remote work can reduce costs associated with employee turnover, absenteeism, and healthcare expenses. Employees who work in sustainable remote environments tend to report higher job satisfaction, better work-life balance, and lower levels of stress-related illness. These factors translate directly into reduced recruitment and training costs, lower healthcare premiums, and improved productivity.

Employee retention becomes a significant economic factor in remote work environments. The cost of replacing a skilled employee can range from 50% to 200% of their annual salary, depending on the role and industry. Sustainable remote work practices that improve employee satisfaction and well-being can significantly reduce turnover costs. The economic benefits of remote work extend beyond individual organizations to include broader societal benefits. Reduced commuting leads to lower transportation costs, reduced environmental impact, and improved traffic conditions. These benefits, while not directly captured by individual organizations, contribute to overall economic efficiency and social well-being. The concept of "economic resilience" becomes important for organizations implementing remote work. Remote work offers developers and teams flexibility, autonomy, and global reach but these advantages can also hide serious risks. In a world without fixed working hours or shared office walls, it's dangerously easy to slip into unsustainable habits. A culture of constant availability, blurred boundaries, and quiet overwork can slowly erode a team's health, creativity, and cohesion. Chapter Ten explores how distributed teams can design long-term resilience operationally, economically, and emotionally by building systems that protect people as much as productivity.

Sustainability in remote work is not just a moral imperative; it's a business one. Burnout, disengagement, and turnover are costly both financially and in terms of lost knowledge and stalled momentum. For collaborative coders in distributed environments, sustainability means more than hitting short-term deadlines. It means fostering a culture that supports healthy habits, prevents overload, and equips people to do their best work not just today, but consistently over time. In a remote setting, this takes careful intention. It's easy for high performers to burn out unnoticed, for deadlines to stretch endlessly across time zones, and for the absence of in-person cues to create blind spots around team fatigue. Leaders must actively counteract these forces with thoughtful systems, transparent communication, and a commitment to human-centered policies.

One of the hidden dangers of distributed work is what many call the "always-on trap." Without a commute to signal the end of the day or a colleague shutting off the lights, developers may feel pressure to remain online far beyond their intended hours. Slack notifications ping late into the evening. Emails are sent across time zones with an implied urgency. Over time, this erodes rest, focus, and motivation. Teams that ignore this slow drift toward overwork find themselves paying the price: slower progress, increased mistakes, and eventually, emotional exhaustion. The antidote is boundary-setting not just for individuals, but for the culture as a whole. Sustainable remote teams make rest visible and respected. They encourage using time-off fully, support asynchronous workflows that don't require immediate responses, and clarify what counts as urgent. They adopt norms like "send later" email scheduling, clear offline indicators, and well-documented handovers so no one feels pressured to be online at all hours. These systems communicate something powerful: your well-being matters as much as your output.

At the organizational level, sustainability also intersects with economic resilience. Remote work can provide a strategic advantage in times of economic downturn, natural disasters, or other disruptions. While traditional office-bound teams may struggle with continuity during crises, remote-capable organizations can remain operational, adaptable, and responsive. This isn't just a theory it's been tested in practice. The COVID-19 pandemic revealed how distributed infrastructures enabled some companies to maintain, and even accelerate, productivity while others were stalled by their dependence on physical office space. But achieving this level of resilience requires more than simply allowing people to work from home. It requires active investment in sustainable practices: robust digital infrastructure, reliable documentation habits, clear team agreements, and ongoing support for remote workers' mental and physical health. These investments yield returns not only in stability, but in innovation. Research consistently shows that employees who are well-rested, mentally supported, and emotionally safe are more likely to contribute creative ideas, collaborate effectively, and drive forward meaningful progress. Sustainability and innovation, in this context, are deeply linked.

A robust economic analysis of remote work must also acknowledge its differential impact across roles and individuals. Not all jobs or people thrive equally in a remote environment. Some roles, particularly those with high collaboration needs or dependent on specialized physical equipment, may struggle outside the office. Others, such as focused engineering or design work, often flourish with uninterrupted time and fewer distractions. Similarly, individual preferences, working styles, and life circumstances play a significant role. A parent managing caregiving responsibilities, a neurodivergent developer needing quiet focus, or a team member living in a region with unstable connectivity may all experience remote work very differently. Sustainable remote organizations account for this diversity. They avoid one-size-fits-all approaches and instead focus on flexibility, empathy, and tailoring support to people's needs. This means offering choice, designing inclusive communication strategies, and ensuring that expectations are clear regardless of where someone sits on the map.

Leadership plays a critical role in this equation. In distributed teams, where stress signals can't be seen across a cubicle wall, leaders must go further to detect and prevent burnout. Regular one-on-ones become essential not just to check progress, but to ask the deeper questions: How are you feeling? What's working for you right now? What's not? These conversations create psychological safety, allowing people to speak up when they're overwhelmed or under-supported. Beyond words, leaders must model sustainable behavior themselves. Taking breaks, stepping away from the keyboard, and being vocal about time off signal to others that rest isn't just allowed it's encouraged. Team agreements around communication windows, meeting-free days, and realistic sprint planning reinforce this, aligning daily rhythms with long-term health.

The tools and rituals of remote work can either support sustainability or undermine it. Thoughtful use of technology plays a key role. Project management systems that offer clarity, async-first communication platforms that reduce meeting overload, and documentation that prevents knowledge silos all contribute to a smoother, less stressful work environment. Equally important is resisting the temptation to overload teams with tools. Tool sprawl increases cognitive load and creates confusion, not productivity. Sustainable teams focus on mastering a few integrated systems well, reducing context switching and making it easier for everyone to stay aligned without constant pings or panic.

Another critical element of long-term sustainability is the pacing of work. In the rush to show that remote teams can "keep up," some organizations lean into aggressive delivery cycles and overly ambitious timelines. But overextension is not proof of success, it's a warning sign. Teams that run too hot for too long eventually break down. Sustainable pacing means setting goals that stretch, not strain. It means recognizing when to slow down, invest in refactoring or documentation, or take time to onboard new teammates properly. It also means honoring the principle that sometimes, doing less is how you ultimately achieve more.

Burnout, when it happens, rarely begins with one major event. It's a cumulative process, a missed lunch here, a late-night message there, a creeping feeling that no matter how much you do, it's never enough. In remote environments, this slow drain is especially dangerous because it often goes unnoticed until it's advanced. The best way to fight burnout isn't with one policy, it's with a culture. A culture that normalizes self-care, that rewards thoughtfulness over speed, that values emotional intelligence as much as technical skill. A culture where asking for help is seen as strength, not weakness.

Finally, it's important to understand that sustainability is not a static goal, it's an ongoing practice. The conditions of remote work evolve new technologies emerge, personal circumstances shift, economic pressures change. What worked six months ago may no longer serve your team today. That's why continuous reflection and adaptation are key. Regular retrospectives focused on process, well-being, and team dynamics, not just output help teams make necessary adjustments. Leadership should treat remote work not as a solved problem, but as a living system that needs tuning, care, and vision.

The true power of remote work lies not just in where people sit, but in how they're supported. When organizations build remote cultures that respect human limits, invest in thoughtful systems, and promote both flexibility and focus, they don't just prevent burnout, they unlock better work. Collaborative coders who are energized, emotionally safe, and sustainably paced are better equipped to innovate, solve hard problems, and grow together over time. As the landscape of work continues to evolve, sustainability is no longer a luxury, it's the foundation of every successful, resilient, and enduring remote team.

www.ingramcontent.com/pod-product-compliance
Lightning Source LLC
Chambersburg PA
CBHW021214250926
51852CB00006B/8